NORTH NORFO

A Portrait in Old Picture Postcards

by

Barrie King

John Nickalls Publications

Dedicated to my partner, Christine, in appreciation of her help and support in producing this book.

First published in 2002 by John Nickalls Publications
Oak Farm Bungalow, Sawyers Lane, Suton,
Wymondham, Norfolk, NR18 9SH
Telephone/Fax: 01953 601893

ISBN 1 904136 08 7

Typeset and Printed by Geo. R. Reeve Ltd.
9-11 Town Green, Wymondham,
Norfolk, NR18 0BD
Telephone: 01953 602297

CONTENTS

CONTENTS *(Continued)*

Abbreviations used in text: c. = circa   p.u. = postally used

ACKNOWLEDGEMENTS

This book could not have been made possible without the help of friends and private collectors for their expert knowledge, help and postcard material. The author would like to thank the following people.

Mr. Eric Reading (Mundesley)
Mr. Gerald Lamont (Fakenham)
Mr. Geoff Breese (West Runton)
Mr. Philip Standley (Wymondham)
Mrs. Rhoda Bunn (Wymondham)
Mr Philip West (Hindringham)
Mr. John Finn (Fakenham)
Mr. Allan Hurn (Cromer)
Mr. J. F. Peake (Blakeney)
The Rev. P. J. Gandon (Hindolveston)

INTRODUCTION

The postcards illustrated in this book start at Happisburgh, which is situated east of Mundesley. We continue from there along the coast to Cromer, taking in coastal villages until reaching Burnham Overy Staithe. Our journey then turns southwards to towns and villages further inland and finally ends in the village of Witton Bridge, a short distance from where we first commenced. Some of the towns we will be visiting are Fakenham, Holt, Aylsham and North Walsham. Most of the postcards shown in this book are from my own private collection, others are loaned from friends and fellow collectors. We all share the same love of collecting and have travelled many miles to postcard fairs in different parts of the country in order to purchase cards on the various themes and areas in which we are most interested.

It is perhaps the nostalgic appeal which draws many people into postcard collecting, we all like to look back into the past and there is no better way to do this than with old postcards. One can choose a year, street, or even a memorable event which happened at a particular time. Having been a collector myself for many years and born in Fakenham, I tend to concentrate on this area and the surrounding towns and villages, although North Norfolk has a wealth of beautiful scenery which lends itself to be the subject of postcards.

Most towns and villages have changed enormously since the first official postcards were introduced by the Swiss and British Post Offices on 1 October 1870, a date which coincided with the first day of issue of the halfpenny postage stamp in Great Britain. Throughout our journey through North Norfolk you will see these changes in the places depicted.

On a final note, I hope that the readers of this book will gain as much pleasure from viewing it as I have done from its compilation.

Barrie King
Fakenham, 2002

HAPPISBURGH LIFEBOAT, c. 1920
The *Jacob and Rachel Valentine*

The *Jacob and Rachel Valentine* was a self-righting lifeboat which operated in Happisburgh from 1907 to 1926. The lifeboat is seen being hauled up the slipway by a team of horses towards the lifeboat station. After the station closed in 1926, it was used as a coastguard lookout until 1935, eventually being demolished in 1955.

HAPPISBURGH BEACH, c. 1905

Three ladies and two gentlemen pose for the photographer dressed in their Edwardian outfits, complemented by the ladies' large hats. One cannot imagine that they were about to embark on a boat trip in this attire. The card was almost certainly published by a local photographer.

HAPPISBURGH LIFEBOAT AND HORSES, c. 1920

A lifeboat station was established at Happisburgh in 1866, and the lifeboat house erected at the same time. This somewhat unusual postcard shows the teamsters mounted and a 10-horse team hitched up to the lifeboat ready to make the hard journey up the cliff top to the lifeboat house. The bottom half of this card shows the boat being pulled up on to the carriage. Note the sea drogue at the front of the boat, which is used for stabilizing purposes at sea.

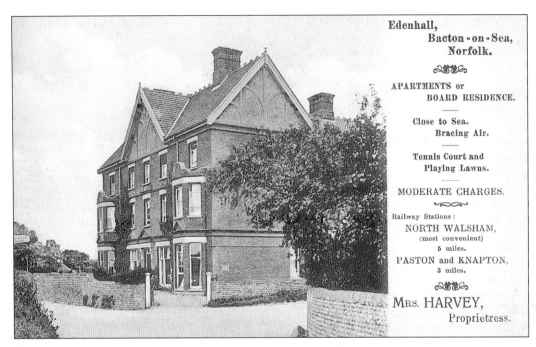

Edenhall,
Bacton - on - Sea,
Norfolk.

APARTMENTS or
BOARD RESIDENCE.

Close to Sea.
Bracing Air.

Tennis Court and
Playing Lawns.

MODERATE CHARGES.

Railway Stations :
NORTH WALSHAM,
(most convenient)
5 miles.
PASTON and KNAPTON,
3 miles.

Mrs. HARVEY,
Proprietress.

EDENHALL, BACTON, c. 1922

Built in the late nineteenth century, it was originally known as Eden Lodge. In 1904, the proprietress was a Mrs. Dixon, followed by Mrs. Harvey around 1922, when it became the Edenhall. Throughout the years, it became a very popular hotel for holiday makers with many facilities as advertised on this postcard. The name then changed once again to Eden Hall Private Hotel, proprietor Mr. W. Davis (1929), and later came under the ownership of Mr. S. Brigg. During the Second World War it was used by various military personnel, being finally demolished in the mid 1990's.

Post Office, Bacton-on-Sea. J 5648. (*Webster's Series.*)

BACTON POST OFFICE, c. 1920

Bacton village Post Office was run by Mr. George Webster, who was also the local draper and patent medicine vendor. In 1905, he was in partnership with a Mr. Haggith. During this time they were involved in other business activities, such as grocers, drapers, a boot and shoe warehouse and fancy repository. The gentleman standing in the doorway may well be Mr. Webster, who was also the publisher of this postcard.

ALFRED LARTER, MUNDESLEY, c. 1925

The shop and apartments were originally built for Mr. Charles Coles in 1890. They were subsequently taken over by Newson & Larter, provision merchants, at the turn of the 20th century. When this picture postcard was taken at around 1925, the proprietor was Alfred Larter. The shops have now been refurbished and are occupied by Spar food stores.

MUNDESLEY COAST GUARD STATION, c. 1908

The coast guards' houses and watchhouse were built at the end of the Napoleonic period. The watchhouse was demolished in 1926 and replaced by the present building, which is now a maritime museum and coastwatch station.

MUNDESLEY SEWER PIPES, c. 1908

A large expanse of water is visible between the end of the sewer pipe and the shoreline. Five men can be seen working on removing the old wood supports ready to lay the new ones for the sewer pipe extension down to the sea. This must have been very hard work, as they had only a limited time to complete each job inbetween the tides.

REPAIRING SEWER-OUTFALL AT MUNDESLEY, c. 1908

Workmen and children pose for the photographer beside a piledriver which is being used for driving in supports for the new sewer pipe. Unlike the mechanical pile drivers of today, this one was manually operated by workmen having to haul the heavy weight up to the top on a pulley before releasing it. The work was carried out by J. Dewbery & Sons, Contractors from Wisbech. In more recent years the sewer pipe was extended due to the increase in population. Notice the lady to the right of the picture standing dangerously close to the tower.

Repairing Sewer-outfall at Mundesley   J. Dewsbery & Son,
                                              Contractors, Wisbech

THE OVERSTRAND HOTEL, c. 1930

The hotel was one of the largest buildings in Overstrand. Sadly it was destroyed by fire around 1948 and was later completely demolished by Easter Brothers of Norwich. Mr. G. Breese, who kindly loaned me this card, used bricks from the Overstrand Hotel to build his bungalow at East Runton. Every single brick was hand cleaned by Mr. Breese senior, (Mr. J. Breese). Approximately 10,000 bricks were used at a cost of £2. 10s. per 1,000.

OVERSTRAND HIGH STREET, c. 1910

Looking down Overstrand High Street, the scene is quite a contrast to the present day, with the absence of cars and lorries. The ladies taking a walk seem quite undeterred by the cattle being driven towards them. In the background is the Overstrand Hotel, the flint building to the right of the picture is Ivy Farm.

GROMER LIFEBOAT   A J ROGERS PHOTO

***LOUISA HEARTWELL*, c. 1902**

The crew of the *Louisa Heartwell* lined up on the lifeboat for this picture, which was taken around 1902. The large wooden boards fitted round the rear wheels of the lifeboat carriage were called Tipping wheelplates, invented by a Mr. T. H. Gartside-Tipping. These plates enabled the carriage to move more easily over the sand by spreading the weight. *Louisa Heartwell* was named by Lady Suffield on 9th September, 1902 and served until 15th May, 1931.

**CREW OF THE LIFEBOAT *LOUISA HEARTWELL*
CROMER, c. 1902**

Left to right back row: Walter "Kite" Rix, Henry Blogg, John "Pokey" Balls, Tom Blyth, Bob Young,
Dinger Blogg, George "Cossey" Nockells, George Wakefield, Walter "Cant" Allen, Bob "Rumbolt" Balls.
Centre row: Tom Kirby, George "Buckeran" Balls, Gilbert "Lentner" Rook, James "Buttons" Harrison
(Coxswain), John Cox, George " Old Dinger" Blogg.
Front row: George "Blinker" Stimpson, James Harrison, Bob Rix.

BROUGHT BACK BY CROMER LIFEBOAT, c. 1912

St. Antoine de Padoue was a fishing boat from Nieuport, Belgium, which was stranded on Haisborough Sands. The crew of 21 seamen managed to reach Haisborough Light Ship in their own ship's boat. They were later picked up by the *Louisa Heartwell* and taken back to Cromer on 29th August, 1912. Surrounded by many local people this picture was taken in the Red Lion yard, Cromer.

CROMER LIFEBOAT, *HARRIOT DIXON* AND CREW

Left to right: Frank Davies, Leslie "Yacker" Harrison, Joe Linder (No. 2 Mechanic), George Cox, Henry "Shrimp" Davies, Billy "Plimpo" Davies, Jimmy Davies, Jack Davies, Leslie Harrison, William "Captain" Davies, Henry Blogg (Coxwain), Tom "Bussey" Allen, Robert "Skinback" Cox, Arthur Balls, Walter Burgess, George Balls, Bob Davies.

Cromer Life-Boat "Ruby and Arthur Reid" PN 5524

P.A. Vicary, Cromer

THE *RUBY AND ARTHUR REID*, c. 1949

A spectacular launching of *The Ruby and Arthur Reid* taking place from No. 1 Lifeboat Station, Cromer. Built by W. Osborne at a cost of £60,000, the lifeboat first came into service at Cromer on March 14th, 1967, and was finally replaced in 1985 by a much faster and more modern boat of the same name. During her time at Cromer she rescued 58 lives and was launched at least 125 times.

CROMER FISHERMAN, c. 1906

From left to right: Kirby, Brackenbury, Sailor Allen, Rook, Pond. The message on the reverse of this card was written by a young lady from London taking a holiday in Cromer. Her message ends by saying, "I thought you might like this card for your collection and please do not think that they are all my fancy chaps will you?"

CROMER CO–OPERATIVE SOCIETY LIMITED, c. 1904

This postcard is a very rare and fine example of a Co–operative Branch shop front which was in Prince of Wales road. The gentleman standing in the doorway is Mr. Percy Scotcher, the branch manager, with his staff, who are wearing long white aprons of the day. On the reverse of this card, which was sent by Mr. Scotcher to a relative, the message reads, "I will send you a parcel this week and please take note of my business expression in this picture". The premises are now occupied by a Suntan Centre.

BOWER'S STEAM BAKERY, CROMER, c. 1908

James Bower was a baker and confectioner with two shops in Cromer. The steam bakery pictured above was located in Church Street with a restaurant and had accommodation for visitors to the town during the holiday season. The second shop was in Garden Street, which had private furnished apartments for rent, known as Fern House.

J. BOWER, CROMER, c. 1910

Showing the two shops of J. Bower, Baker and Confectioner. This postcard was probably published by Mr. Bower and either given away or sold from his shops as a means of advertising.

J. BOWER, Baker and Confectioner, CHURCH STREET AND GARDEN STREET, CROMER.

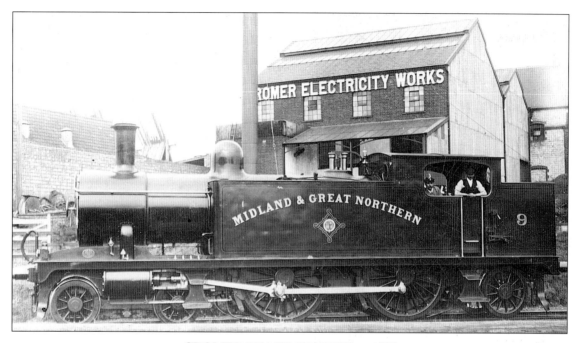

CROMER BEACH STATION, c. 1929

The No. 9 engine of the Midland & Great Northern Railway stands in front of the Cromer Electricity Works at Beach station. The station was first used in 1887 by Eastern & Midlands Railways. In 1956, there were 14 trains a day running between Norwich Thorpe and Beach station for passengers to and from the coast. Rationalization came and by February 1959 the passenger service ceased. The station retained its goods facilities for a few more years before finally closing, when a new purpose built coal yard was erected on the site of the old Victoria station Norwich.

CROMER, SHUNTING ENGINE, c. 1919

The two gentlemen posing for this photograph are seen proudly showing the *Alpha* shunting engine. The *Alpha* M. & G.N. works shunter is pictured near Roughton during the building of the No. 5 line to Mundesley.

CROMER STATION, c.1920

Cromer station was situated quite a long way from the sea front and was one of the busiest on the Norfolk coast. Closing in 1954, the trains and passengers were diverted to Cromer Beach station. The large building to the right of the main platform was the engine shed with a water tank on top. Today, the site is occupied by a new housing development.

MARLBOROUGH HOTEL, CROMER, c. 1904

The Marlborough Hotel was situated on Prince of Wales Road and was typical of Victorian architecture, with large bay windows and an ornate turret positioned on the roof above the entrance. Inside was a dance floor of sprung Maplewood, which was very luxurious at the time. During the Second World War, soldiers were billeted in the rooms. Sadly it was demolished in the 1950's and a petrol station now occupies the site.

CROMER, c. 1911

The boys are standing to attention for the Review of the Boys' Brigade at Beef Meadow, Cromer on 5th June, 1911. Mr. H. Douglas-King is the inspecting officer and is dressed in the Royal Navy uniform of a Lieutenant.

CABBELL PARK, CROMER, c. 1938

Cabbell Park and football ground has played host to many big events over the years. This postcard is advertising a travelling show known as "Les Cosaques Djiguites" – ("The Fearless Horsemen") and claiming to be *The Worlds Most Daring Display*. At the time this must have been quite a show for the people of Cromer.

CROMER URBAN DISTRICT.

BYE-LAWS
AS TO
PUBLIC BATHING

The following are the appointed Stands for Bathing Machines.

No. of Stand.	Description or limits of Stand.	Sex to which appropriated.
1	Between the Doctor's Steps Groyne and the Cart Gangway - - - - -	FEMALE
2	Between the Doctor's Steps Groyne and a point 100 yards to the East thereof—	
	Before the hour of 8 a.m. daily - -	MALE
	After the hour of 8 a.m. daily - -	MALE & FEMALE
3	To the East of a point 200 yards to the East of the Doctor's Steps Groyne, being 100 yards East of the Easternmost limit of Stand No. 2 - - - - -	MALE
4	To the West of Melbourne House Groyne—	
	Before the hour of 8 a.m. daily - -	MALE
	After the hour of 8 a.m. daily - -	MALE & FEMALE

GENTLEMEN bathing in the Mixed Bathing Ground must wear a suitable costume, from neck to knee.

Copies of the Bye-laws may be obtained at the Offices of the Council. Persons offending against the Bye-laws are liable to a Penalty of £5.

By Order,

P. E. HANSELL,

Cromer, April, 1898.   *Clerk to the District Council.*

BATHING LAWS, CROMER, c. 1898

A postcard reproduced from a poster which was used to state the laws of male and female bathing areas along the beach. Members of the public who did not adhere to the byelaws were liable to a £5 fine, which was quite a large sum of money to pay in 1898.

GOLF CLUB HOUSE, CROMER.

GOLF CLUB HOUSE, CROMER, c.1919

Local farmer, Mr. Robert le Neve, built a wood and corrugated iron lock-up shop in West Street and started a butchers business. When the business closed, the building was purchased by the Royal Cromer Golf Club in 1890. It was then dismantled and transported to "Happy Valley" for use as a club house. The centre of the building showing two Chinese style gables was the original building and the extensions at each end were added later.

Roman Camp, Near Cromer.

THE ROMAN CAMP, NEAR CROMER, c. 1927

The Roman Camp is located near Cromer just off the A148. Being a place of natural beauty with tea gardens and wooded walks, it is much used by the locals and holiday makers during the summer months. The Camp, owned by the National Trust, is the site of an Anglo-Saxon iron working settlement and is the highest point in Norfolk at approximately 328ft.

ABBS BROTHERS EAST RUNTON BUS, c. 1920

One of the Abbs brothers of East Runton with their open top bus surrounded by billboards advertising trips to local towns and villages. The board displays today's trips starting 2.30 at Blakeney Harbour via Weybourne, Cley – staying 1/2 hour. Returning home by Bayfield Park, Holt, Pretty Corner and stopping for tea at the Roman Camp – fare: two shillings and sixpence. This trip in the 1920's was probably considered as quite a days outing. In between running Saturday and Sunday outings, the brothers were proprietors of two wet fish shops, one being in Runton and the other in Sheringham.

FISHERMEN, EAST RUNTON.

EAST RUNTON FISHERMEN, c. 1909
Six hardy East Runton fishermen line up with their crab pots and boat. *Left to right:* Steve Green, Dardy Love, Bob Love, Arthur Gray, Nip Tuck, Mat Love.

BEESTON ROAD, SHERINGHAM, c. 1912

Beeston Road remains much the same today as it did when this picture was taken. The presence of a horse and cart, gas street lamp and lovely dress fashions of the day takes us back in time to a typical street scene of bygone days.

SHERINGHAM HIGH STREET, c. 1910

Sheringham High Street must be the most photographed of all in the town. Although it has changed greatly over the years, the town reservoir remains the same but for a clock which has been mounted on top. Built in 1862, it supplied the town with water from local springs. The clock is known as "The Mary Pymm", being named after the lady who presented it to Sheringham in 1903. The trough in the reservoir was used during the First World War, when troops stationed in the area watered their horses.

High Street, Sheringham.

HIGH STREET, SHERINGHAM, c.1920

Looking towards the clock in the distance we see the opposite view of the High Street. Eastman's Limited, Family Butchers, are on the right and Starling's Newsagents to the left of the picture. Note the milk churn and cart outside the Norfolk Dairy Company.

SHERINGHAM FISHERMEN

One of many photographs taken of Sheringham fishermen. *Left to right:* "Sixy" Knowles, Bennet, Young "Coaley" Cooper, George "Hammond" Grice, Old "Coaley" Cooper, Jimmy Dumble.

BOILING WHELKS, SHERINGHAM, c. 1914

Prior to the First World War, Sheringham had a thriving trade in whelks. The leading fish merchant was a Mr. Harry Johnson who bought whelks from the fishermen, boiled them and sold them on the open market. He was at one time the owner of five whelk coppers in Sheringham. The whelk industry ceased just before the Second World War.

GUNS, WEYBOURNE CAMP J & S 1284

WEYBOURNE CAMP, c. 1939

Anti-aircraft guns point out to sea at Weybourne Camp. During World War II, this part of the coast was home to as many as 1,300 servicemen at one time. It became the Anti-Aircraft Permanent Range and Radar Training Wing, giving instruction to the many national servicemen that passed through the camp. It is estimated that at least 1,500,000 shells had been fired at targets in the air and on sea. The camp closed in 1959, and was mostly returned to agricultural land. Today, the original NAAFI remains and is home to the Muckleburgh Collection, a wonderful museum of armoured cars, tanks and amphibious vehicles from battlefields all over the world.

THE WINDMILL, CLEY-NEXT-TO-SEA, c. 1920

Dominating the centre of the village and situated on the edge of the river Glaven stands Cley windmill. Built as a cornmill in the early 18th century, it ceased work in 1919. John Lee was recorded as the first tenant miller in 1822, being in business as a maltster and corn merchant. Mr John Farthing, owner of the mill died in 1848 and the mill was then taken over by William Edward Powell who was the second tenant miller (1850). He was succeeded by Lawrence Randell (1853–1872), after his retirement a Mr. Stephen Barnabas Burroughes took over the business. Mr. Burroughes was a baker at Langham and Holt (1875–1896). The mill was owned at this time by Mrs. Dorothy Farthing, who died shortly after the last tenant moved in. After Mrs. Farthing died the mill was sold at auction. In 1983, the present owner (Mr. Charles Blount) was granted planning permission to use it as a guest house and it received its first guests on 27th April. The mill has been used in quite a few films including "Conflict of Wings", starring John Gregson.

GLANDFORD MILL, c. 1907

Glandford Mill, which stands on the River Glaven, was at one time owned by Sir Alfred Jodrell. Sir Alfred who lived in Bayfield Hall, Holt was well known in the area for his generosity, which included sending produce weekly to kitchens of the Norfolk and Norwich Hospital. The wording on the cart standing in the barn reads "Sir A. Jodrell Bart – Glaven Rollermills, Glandford". The mill is now a private residence.

Blakeney Quay.   J. C. Parker's Series.

BLAKENEY HARBOUR, c. 1907

Blakeney Harbour was well situated for sheltering small ships and, in 1817, was vastly improved through an Act of Parliament to allow vessels of 150 tons to approach the quay. There was at one time a thriving oyster industry which employed as many as 100 ships. On an area called the Carnser, pits were used up until 1912 to store and clean oysters and mussels, eventually closing down around 1921. The main ship owners at the turn of the century were Page and Turner, who owned the only steam boat to come into Blakeney quay as the majority of vessels were sailing ships. *Taffy* was the name of this steam boat, a 73 ton vessel registered at Runcorn.

LABORATORY, BLAKENEY POINT c. 1930

Dr. F. W. Oliver (later Professor) University College London was closely involved with research on Blakeney Point, which continues to this day. Dr. Oliver's interest had started before the Point came under the guardianship of the National Trust, in fact he had obtained permission from Lord Calthorpe to develop a "marine garden" at the Point. To further research, Dr. Oliver developed various facilities on the Point and one of these was the Laboratory. It continued to be used for this purpose until comparatively recently. Today, it still remains and is used as a bunkhouse for students.

Houseboat, Britannia, Blakeney Point

84382.

HOUSEBOAT, BRITANNIA, BLAKENEY POINT, c. 1912

Boats of all kinds and sizes, including hulls, were moored in the harbour on the Point side of the channel. These were used by various people, the more luxurious boats like this one were hired out as family holiday boats, others were used by fishermen and the first warden (Mr. Pinchin) who also used one moored in what was to become known as "Pinchin's Creek".

STIFFKEY, c. 1905

Today, Stiffkey is almost a mile from the sea, but at one time it had its own harbour. The postcard shows a band of cockle gatherers, most of whom appear to be ladies. It must have been very hard work indeed. I know from experience that cockles are very heavy when gathered in quantity. Stiffkey has been famous for its cockles for many years, known locally as "STEWKY BLUES". Few remain today, especially after the 1953 coastal floods. Note the heavy sacks on the backs of the lady and the gentleman in the picture.

REV. H. DAVIDSON M. A.
WELL KNOWN AS THE RECTOR OF STIFFKEY,
PHOTOGRAPHED AT THE FAMOUS BARREL EXHIBITION BLACKPOOL 1933.
PHOTO BY SALOMAN, BROS. BLACKPOOL.

THE VICAR OF STIFFKEY, c. 1933

The Rev. H. Davidson, M.A. was well known as the Vicar of Stiffkey. He was very respected by the people of Stiffkey and Morston. Sadly he had one great weakness, the ladies, and this was to eventually lead to his downfall. He claimed that he was the prostitutes padre and that he saved them from the streets of London. After a lot of scandal and press reports, he was finally defrocked. He then went on the music halls and a series of seaside arcades and side shows, telling of his slander, disgrace and downfall. One of his acts was to roll the length of Blackpool promenade in a barrel. This postcard shows him posing at the famous Barrel Exhibition at Blackpool in 1933. On 28th July, 1937, while performing with lions in a cage at Skegness Amusement Park, he was badly mauled and later died of his wounds. He was Rector of Stiffkey and Morston for 26 years and is buried in Stiffkey churchyard.

VICAR OF STIFFKEY PUBLICITY CARD

The Reverend Davidson published these cards himself and handed them out to close friends and to people of Stiffkey and Morston. The idea of doing this was to try and convince the public of his innocence. This card has his signature on the reverse.

WELLS REGATTA, c. 1922

Crowds gather along the quay wall for the 1922 Regatta to watch various sailing and rowing races. The first Regatta in Wells was held in 1859, marking the opening of the beach bank and has continued to the present day. Contestants also participated in swimming races and races in barrels, one very amusing favourite was the greasy pole. In 1869 a pig had its tail greased and was then set free to run over the marsh and creeks, after a long chase the gentleman who managed to catch it was not only the winner but the proud owner of a pig.

Floods 1953 at Wells, Norfolk.

Acock Series 4.

FLOODS AT WELLS, *(The Terra Nova)*, **1953**

High and dry on Wells quay, 3rd February, 1953, is the *Terra Nova* motor torpedo boat after water surged over the quayside during the east coast floods. Local man Mr. Billy Tuffs was working in a quayside fish and chip shop at the time and saw the boat approaching the fish shop side-on, a sight which will always remain with him. The *Terra Nova*, a Sea Scouts Training Ship was later relaunched without any serious damage. It ended its days moored up the east end of the channel until finally being destroyed by fire between 1953–55.

10,171 The Beach House, Wells

THE BEACH HOUSE, WELLS-NEXT-THE-SEA, c. 1933

The Beach House (often referred to as the Jubilee Tea Rooms) served teas and ice cream to the many holiday-makers that came to Wells in the 20's and 30's. Mr. George Frederick Finn, who sold confectionery from a stall on the left of the picture, also had two more tea stalls on the beach. These stalls were open only in the summer months with the main shop premises located in 35 Staithe Street. The Jubilee Tea Rooms were later taken over by Mr. Finn around the time this picture was taken. Mr. George Sarsby was the carpenter who erected the confectionery stall. Mr. Finn ceased trading around 1938-39 and this area, having been virtually destroyed during the 1953 floods, is now a large car park.

FISH AND CHIPS AT WELLS-NEXT-THE-SEA, c. 1912

Mr. George Frederick Finn (senior) with his mobile fish and chip shop. This picture is thought to have been taken in Theatre Road; from left to right is Mr. George Frederick Finn, Mr. Oscar Cubitt, George Frederick Finn (junior) and Mr. Syd "Crotchy" Smith. The business was eventually carried on by Mr. Finn junior's son, Mr. John Finn and later in turn handed over to John's son in 1995 – Mr. Spencer Finn.

G. F. FINN, WELLS-NEXT-THE-SEA, c. 1912

A wonderful example of an ice cream salesman with his handcart. Mr. Tom Frost, also known by the locals as "Tom Thumb", sold ice creams around Wells during the summer season for Mr. George Frederick Finn.

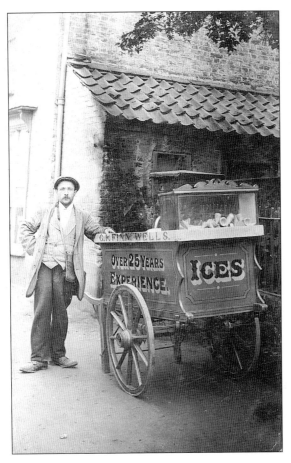

THE BEACH HOUSE
WELLS-NEXT-THE-SEA, c. 1905

Wells Beach House was leased by a Mrs. Wooltorton around 1890. The large display of cycles which are parked at the rear of the building gives an indication of what was the most common means of transport to and from the beach on hot summer days. An advertising announcement in the Wells Herald of 1890 stated that: "The Beach House is situated at the end of the new bank within twenty minutes of the railway station. Mrs. Wooltorton has determined that, while everything shall be first-class, there shall be none of the extortionate charging common to many watering places."

MRS. WOOLTORTON'S TEA STALL
WELLS-NEXT-THE-SEA, c. 1905

Pictured above is a tea stall located on the beach run by Mrs. Wooltorton who had a confectioners and tea room in the High Street at Wells. Mr. and Mrs. Wooltorton were also involved in other business activities such as bill posting, bathing tent and boat hire, swings and rocking horses, which were situated on the beach. The tea stall advertised sandwiches freshly cut daily at 2d. each and tea or coffee at 1½d. per cup.

OVERY STAITHE, c. 1952

Looking towards the boathouse, this view shows the stretch of road which is very often flooded at the time of high tides. The boathouse, which dates back to 1840, was originally a granary. It is now in the care of a private company called Burnham Overy Boathouse Limited. All profits from the boathouse and chandlery business are ploughed back in, to secure and maintain the building and keep it in its original form. Improvements to the building are very carefully considered before being carried out. Mr. Coutanche, the present manager, succeeds Mr. Peter Beck who was at the helm for 41 years. Another more notable resident of Overy Staithe was Captain Woodget, Master of the famous clipper *Cutty Sark* who lived at Flagstaff House from 1910 to 1926 and is buried in Norton churchyard.

THE WINDMILL, OVERY STAITHE, c.1927

Overy Staithe mill stands in a most prominent position with uninterrupted views across the marshes towards the north sea. The mill is a tarred brick windmill built by Edmund Savory in 1816. Remaining in the Savory family until around 1900, it was then sold to Mr. Sidney F. Dewing. The windmill finally stopped working in 1919 and, in 1958, it was given to the National Trust who restored and converted it to residential accommodation to be let out all year round to visitors to the area.

OVERY STAITHE MILL INTERIOR, c. 1920

A very rare and unusual postcard of the interior of Burnham Over Staithe Mill. Having six floors, this comfortable circular room with extremely large beam work was most probably situated on the second or third floor.

MARKET PLACE, BURNHAM MARKET

No. 1465

BURNHAM MARKET WAR MEMORIAL, c. 1930

After the First World War ended, it was decided that a war memorial should be erected in memory of the local men who gave their lives for freedom. The memorial was placed opposite what used to be Mr. Whites chemist shop, in the centre of the market place at a cost of £262. 12s. 5d. On Sunday, 17th October, 1920, Lord Leicester unveiled the memorial, accompanied by a very large crowd. Thirty-four Burnham Market men were killed in the 1914-18 war and sadly the list was added to by those who fell in the Second World War.

BURNHAM MARKET BUTCHER, c. 1910

This fine study of a social history card shows Arthur Robert Wilson's butchers delivery vehicle with the driver and assistant. The shop was situated at the west end of Burnham Market near Herrings Lane in an area known as Market Stalls. When Mr. Wilson ceased trading in 1923, the shop was taken over by Snelling Brothers family butchers, who ran the business for a number of years. The building has long since been demolished.

BUST OF LORD NELSON
(Burham Thorpe Church)

Burnham Thorpe is famous for having been the birthplace of Admiral Viscount Nelson, Duke of Bronte. He was born on 29th September, 1758. The bust of Lord Nelson pictured on this postcard, can be seen in the church. It was erected in 1905 by the London Society of East Anglians to commemorate the centenary of the Battle of Trafalgar. Later, in 1911, an altar was erected in memory of the men who were killed in action at Trafalgar. A Memorial Hall was erected in 1891, at a cost of £556, as a tribute to the memory of Lord Nelson.

BUST OF LORD NELSON
BURNHAM THORPE CHURCH

BURNHAM THORPE CHURCH

All Saint's Church, Burnham Thorpe is an edifice in the perpendicular style, consisting of a chancel, nave, aisles and a western tower which has one bell. In 1886, there was an oak lecturn installed in the church as a memorial to Lord Nelson. The lecturn was made of wood taken from *H.M.S. Victory* and presented by the Lords of the Admiralty in 1881. In 1905, Sir William John Lancaster donated a pulpit to the church. Lord Nelson's father, the Rev. Edmund Nelson, who was Rector for forty-six years, died on 26th April, 1802.

The Shooting Box, North Creake. 84460

THE SHOOTING BOX, NORTH CREAKE, p.u. 1927

The house known as the Shooting Box in North Creake was demolished some years ago. During World War II, it was used by the Government for the accommodation of land army girls and later used as a radar station in connection with Sculthorpe Aerodrome. Only the stable blocks remain standing today and are occupied by a company called "Kitchens Etc", who specialise in making hand crafted kitchens and bathrooms.

THE BREWERY SOUTH CREAKE

CARTWRIGHT.

THE BREWERY, SOUTH CREAKE, c. 1912

South Creake brewery is said to have been in existence during the reign of George II (1727–1764). On August 28th, 1898 the brewery was badly damaged by fire. The owner at the time was a Mr. James Pinchen, Brewer, Maltster and Mineral Water manufacturer, who also had a brewery at Corpusty. Mr. Pinchen's son journeyed by pony and trap to alert the Fire Brigade at Fakenham but, by the time Fakenham firemen had rigged up the horses to the fire engine and made their way back to Creake, half the brewery had burnt down and the tower was completely destroyed.

SOUTH CREAKE STRING BAND, c. 1911

South Creake Guild String Band, as they were known, are seen here outside the Congregational Church.
They played locally and in many other parts of the County and proved to be very popular in their time.
The band instructor was a Mr. Hubert Mann. Other members of the band were Maud Tyce, Kate Smith
and a Mr. Shackcloth, who was later killed in action during the First World War.

SOUTH CREAKE, c. 1904

South Creake is approximately 6 miles South West of Fakenham. This postcard shows Cartwright's Village Stores and Post Office, which is situated on the west side of the Village Green. It was first owned by the Cartwrights in the early 1800's and since then has changed hands within and outside the family. Llewellyn Cartwright owned it in 1904, Mrs. Sarah Cartwright in 1929. In 1936, it was sold to Mr. Alex Seaman, and then to a Mr. Watts-Russell, eventually returning back to the Seaman family via Mr. Mike Seaman in 1994, who ran a thriving restaurant business and village shop. In 2000, the restaurant was closed, and the shop and premises were sold the following year. This scene is little changed today.

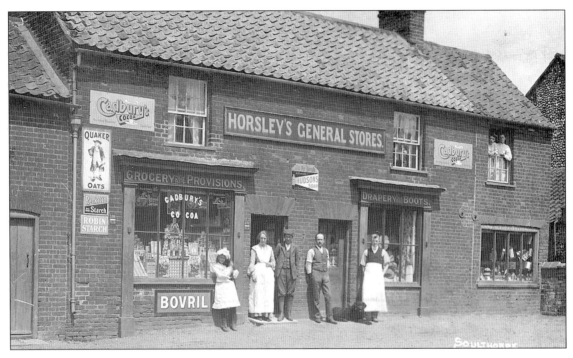

HORSLEY'S STORES, SCULTHORPE, p.u. 1908

Sculthorpe is a village about 2 miles north-west of Fakenham. The village had its own Watermill, situated on the River Wensum, which is now a Public House/Hotel. Horsley's General Stores was in the centre of the village. The Proprietor was a Mrs. Lucy Horsley, who may well be the lady standing in the shop doorway. Like most village shops in the early 1900s, it sold everything required by the local residents.

GOGG'S MILL, HEMPTON, FAKENHAM, c. 1903

There are two mills in Hempton, a watermill and windmill. The oldest was the watermill, which was built around 1720 and derived its name from the owner, Mr. Thomas Goggs. Starting in business at the age of 21, he was the eldest son of the Rev. Henry Goggs and lived in Grove House, Fakenham, where he died in 1913. The mill ceased to operate at the beginning of the First World War. During the 1950's it was completely demolished.

HEMPTON MILL, p.u. 1908

Hempton windmill was first mentioned in historical records in 1827. It was built of bricks made locally on what was known as the Brickground. In 1835, John Jarrett of Abbey Farm left it to his wife, Elizabeth Jarrett, who carried on the business as Corn Miller and Maltster. During the First World War, the windmill was used for storage and no longer for milling. In 1939, the brick tower was still standing and was finally demolished in 1944, during the Second World War. Mill House which stands in front of the windmill's original site, is still in use as a private dwelling today.

HEMPTON, HORNS ROW, p.u. 1905

A delightful card showing people gathered outside the cottages known as Horns Row, which were situated to the right hand side of The Old Buck Inn. Fakenham bypass now runs through the site of the Inn. The cottages above are still there today. Note the sign on the wall: "Pony and Trap for Hire".

**COLKIRK BRANCH OF FAKENHAM
CO-OPERATIVE SOCIETY, c. 1914**

Colkirk Co-operative Society Limited was situated on the right-hand side of School Road as you leave the village towards East Raynham. Pictured in the shop doorway is possibly Mr. Richard Britton, who was for many years Branch Secretary. The shop closed around 1938 and was later demolished. Today the site is occupied by a double garage which adjoins the cottage to the left of the picture. Note the display of gentlemen's braces in the shop window on the right.

RED LION HOTEL, MARKET PLACE, FAKENHAM, c. 1904

The Red Lion Hotel, known earlier as The Lion dates back to Tudor times. The horse and carriage standing in front has the name Red Lion Hotel displayed on its sides. This amongst other trips was probably used to ferry people back and forth from the local railway stations. The Red Lion Hotel closed in 1974 and became local council offices and a Tourist Information office, eventually closing in 2000. The building to the right of the hotel was a bank and is now a branch of Stead & Simpson. Opposite the bank is a music shop belonging to Mr. Joseph Wainwright whose business ceased trading around the 1950's. These premises are now occupied by a fruit and vegetable business.

FAKENHAM MARKET PLACE, c. 1906

This rare card shows a large crowd gathered in the town centre on market day, which may well be the start of a local auction. In the background (right) is Heyhoe's Drug Store and the National Bank of Scotland, which was established in 1833. These two establishments have long been closed and the whole building is now occupied by Boots the Chemists. The Crown Hotel and archway remains the same today. Note the telegram boy to the right of the picture.

FAKENHAM SALVATION ARMY YOUNG PEOPLES BAND, c. 1941

The Young Peoples Band was formed to replace the main members of the band who had been called up for active service during the Second World War. They proved to be highly successful and were very popular in and around Fakenham during the war years. This picture was taken behind what is known today as "The Press Club" in Oak Street. *Left to right back row:* Dick Stewart, John Mitchell, Herbert Woodhouse, Bram Barker, Horace Barnett. *Middle row:* John "Nipper" Heazel, Joy Heazel, Joan Barnett, Maurice Bullock, Bram Jarrett, Major M. Jarrett (Officer in Charge), Eddie Barnett (Band Master), Mrs. Jarrett, Jack Bird, Maurice Bayfield, Victor Edgely, Charlie Dodman, Reggie Dewson. *Front row:* Clifford Edgely, Roy Sayer.

FAKENHAM TOWN FOOTBALL TEAM, c. 1909

Top row, left to right: R. Bannister, L. Syder, G. Salisbury, Fred Beazer, C. Carly (inset).
Second row: C. Powell, H. Croft, Frank Beazer (Captain), J. Shirley, R. Drewell.
Bottom row: W. Millar, C. Gardener *(the authors late uncle).*
Fakenham were winners of the Norfolk Junior Cup in 1900, 1906 and winners of the North Norfolk
League Cup in 1907, 1908, 1909. The message on the reverse of this card reads: "This team was beaten in
the final of the Dereham Challenge Cup by Kings Lynn 4-2".

FAKENHAM FIREMAN, c. 1912

Pictured is Mr. Charlie Wright, who was a member of the Fakenham Fire Brigade. This card was kindly given to me by his grandson, Mr. David Wright. The fire station, built in 1911, was situated in Hall Staithe; although it is not used any more, the building remains unchanged. The present fire station is located in Norwich Road.

FAKENHAM GREAT EASTERN STATION, c. 1905

The Norfolk Railway opened in Fakenham on 20th March, 1849 and was continued on to Wells-next-the-Sea by the Wells and Fakenham Railway on 1st January, 1857. It was later taken over by British Railways and the station became known as Fakenham East. Being a very busy station it was at one time the scene of a train crash. A head on collision occurred in 1931, when an early train from Norwich to Wells collided with a train which was stationary at the platform. Several people were injured, with one passenger being killed. On May 10th, 1964 it was closed to passengers, the goods service being finally closed in 1979. The station was demolished in September 1984, with the goods yard opposite, following in January 1989.

BARSHAM FLOOD DISASTER, c. 1912

This postcard shows the accident at Barsham Bridge which spanned the River Stiffkey. The bridge supports were washed away by the flood waters and collapsed under the weight of the locomotive, bringing the train to a halt by the wagons falling through the damaged section on Monday, 26th August, 1912. This photograph was taken the following day by a local photographer.

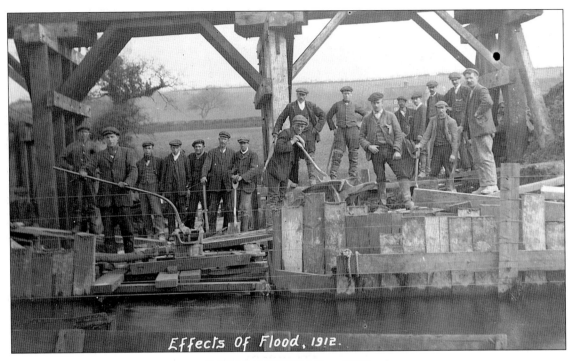

Effects Of Flood, 1912.

BARSHAM BRIDGE, c. 1912

Barsham Bridge being rebuilt after the 1912 August floods. By the 10th September a replacement bridge was erected, allowing the Fakenham to Wells line to be reopened. A large amount of timber was used on the reconstruction of the bridge and the work was carried out by a gang of no less than 17 men.

WALSINGHAM FLOOD RESCUE, c. 1912

The pretty picturesque village of Little Walsingham, lies five miles south of Wells. This picture was taken at the height of the 1912 floods and as we can see, there are four men in the boat including a Police Officer. Photographed at the entrance to Walsingham High Street, they are engaged in rescue work and delivering food supplies. Visitors standing at this spot today would find it hard to imagine what it was like at the time of the floods.

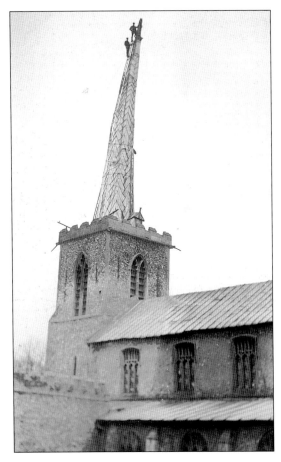

WALSINGHAM, ST MARY'S CHURCH, c. 1905

St. Mary's Church, a 14th-15th century building had a large amount of restoration work carried out in the 1860s by G. E. Street. The bells were cast by William Silisden at around 1330 and are said to be some of the oldest bells in the country. In 1961, it was entirely gutted by fire and rebuilt by a Mr. Laurence King. It appears that in this picture the church spire is badly twisted. The two men perched precariously at the top of the spire have no safety harness, and the gentleman at the very top appears to be holding on with one hand.

GREAT SNORING POST OFFICE

Great Snoring village is located approximately seven miles inland from Wells-next-the-Sea. In the past, the village had two public houses, three shops, a blacksmith and carpenter. An egg packing station owned by Sainsbury's was in operation in Great Snoring from 1936. A Mr. Henry Green was the village sub-postmaster and carpenter in 1904. In 1929, Mr. Thomas Styman was recorded as being sub-postmaster, and he was succeeded by his son John. The shop and post office finally closed in April 1984. One interesting point about the village is that Great Snoring at one time had its own ladies' cricket team.

NORTH ELMHAM POST OFFICE AND VILLAGE STORES, c. 1920

North Elmham Post Office was for a number years owned by the Kerrison family. In 1904, Robert Kerrison was the owner and traded as family grocer, draper, ironmonger, dealer in ammunition and sub-postmaster. Mr. Kerrison finally sold it around 1969. Unlike the majority of village stores which are long gone, the shop and post office continued under one or two other proprietors. Today the business is thriving and well stocked under the ownership of Graham and Rosemary McGreish.

THE SWAN INN, GUIST, c. 1920

Advertising Bullards Ales on its sign to the left, the Swan Inn dates back to the 17th century. Mr. Henry Durham was the landlord in the 1950s and left around 1962. The last landlord was Mr. Henry and Violet Everson who took over in 1963. Sadly it closed around 1984 and is now a privately owned residence.

(South) Market Place, Reepham. 124607.

REEPHAM POST OFFICE, c. 1920

Reepham is approximately 12 miles north-west of Norwich. The post office, which was situated in the market place, was run by a Mr. D. Chapman and Mr. H. Kendall. The shop, which was also a stationery and fancy goods outlet, traded under the name of Kendall Chapman. Records show that a Mrs. Lydia A. Rudd was the previous sub-postmistress. Like the majority of village post offices it finally closed down in the 1930s. Today, the hectagonal shaped building on the left-hand side of the post office is a very attractive catering and coffee shop (Diane's Pantry), and the former post office, a fruit and vegetable shop.

CHURCH HILL ROAD, REEPHAM, c. 1919

A charming rural scene of Reepham village. The post card shows Church Hill Road, although it is captioned Norwich Road, apparently Norwich Road starts further down at the junction. Two of the ladies standing next to the pony and trap are believed to be a Mrs. Basham and her daughter, two well known local residents at the time. Today, this street remains much unchanged.

4942 THE POST OFFICE, HINDOLVESTON.

HINDOLVESTON POST OFFICE, c. 1909

Hindolveston Post Office was first situated in the shop attached to the village bakery. At its height this was a major local business consisting of a mill, the bakery and the baker's house. The sails of the mill ceased to work about 1925, though milling powered by a diesel engine continued for some years later. The last loaf of bread was baked in 1957 and the Post Office and shop closed in 1971. The baker's house and Post Office seen in the picture dates back to 1740. Past postmasters and owners were: Mrs. Anges Bowman, Mr. Orris Pegg, Mr. Davison, Mr. Faulkner and Mr. College. The property is now known as The Old Bakery and is a private residence.

HINDOLVESTON, c. 1919

Hindolveston was at one time commonly called Hilderston or Hindol by the locals. It had a railway station and three public houses, The Chequers, Red Lion and Maid's Head. The railway station ceased to operate in 1959. The building in the background is The Chequers Inn, which is now closed and has become a private dwelling. The cottages to the right of the picture have long since been demolished and a new house now occupies this site. This superb picture of village life shows Hindolveston Brass Band accompanied by some of the locals on Church Parade Day, 1919. Hindolveston Brass Band was founded in 1902 and is still going strong today.

MELTON CONSTABLE STATION, c. 1908

Looking at the station view toward's Kings Lynn, with it being an island platform, two trains could leave each side simultaneously. The first line ran towards Fakenham and King's Lynn, and the second line to Holt, Sheringham, Cromer and Norwich Thorpe. On the other side of the island platform the third line would head towards Hindolveston, Guestwick, Whitwell, Lenwade, Attlebridge, Drayton, Hellesdon and finally Norwich City Station. The fourth one went to Corpusty, Aylsham, North Walsham, Stalham, Potter Heigham, Caister and Yarmouth Beach Station. The three windows on the right were where the first class waiting rooms were located, next was the door to the ladies waiting room, with a full time lady attendant.

MELTON CONSTABLE STATION, c. 1955

The coaling stage can be seen to the right of the engine. From here coal wagons were filled ready to load the tenders of the engine with coal. There were also two water hydrants, one was near the Melton East signal box and the other was located next to Lord Hastings private waiting room at the far end of the station. In the centre of the platform can be seen two small boarded buildings which were the Station Foreman's office and Inspector's office, the second one being the Station Master's office. The station closed around 1959, although freight was operated on the line for some time after that.

Mr. Harold Drewry was the last serving Station Master at Melton Constable.

S 1353   FITTING SHOP, RAILWAY WORKS, MELTON CONSTABLE.

MELTON CONSTABLE RAILWAY WORKS, c. 1920

The railway works was mainly used for repairs and overhauling although sixteen engines were actually built there. This came to an end around 1936, after which most of the fitters and work force went to places like Crewe and Derby. During the war, the fitting shops were used to make ammunition for the war effort, and the last major use for the workshop was for manufacturing tarpaulins for wagons. Today, a company who manufacture electrical resistors occupy the premises.

BRISTON ROAD, MELTON CONSTABLE, c. 1908

Briston Road, Melton has changed very little since this picture was taken. The first corner shop was a bakery owned by a Mr. Rose and later taken over by Mr. Jack Gaskin. The next corner shop behind the two trees was a butchers run by a Mr. Stalham, this later became a freezer shop which eventually closed and is now a private dwelling. All the houses on the right hand side as you come down the hill were railway houses and the ones on the left were mostly privately owned.

HOLT, c. 1955

Holt is a thriving town situated 12 miles South East of Fakenham. At one time it had its own market, but sadly this closed in the 1960's. On the left in this scene is the Feathers Hotel, which in the past, was home to a variety of businesses, including the Inland Revenue, Corn Merchants and Post Office. It also held cattle sales in the rear yard. The High Street remains much the same today, except for the obvious absence of double yellow lines and traffic wardens.

HOLT WAR MEMORIAL, c. 1929

People gathered round Holt War Memorial for what was probably a Remembrance Sunday. Children from the "Start Point" private school can be seen in the centre of the picture, with Robinsons garaged featured in the background. Today, this building, which has the Railway Tavern to the left, is occupied by four shop units, including Holt Tourist Information office.

HOLT, c. 1915

These soldiers are possibly members of the 6th Battalion (Cyclists), the Royal Sussex Regiment. At about two o'clock on the morning of the 11th August 1915, the residents of Holt were awakened by a large force of Territorials who arrived on cycles, accompanied by numerous motor cars. Quarters were quickly established for them in the halls and schools of the town, the officers making their headquarters at the Feathers Hotel. It was understood that they would remain in the town for some time.

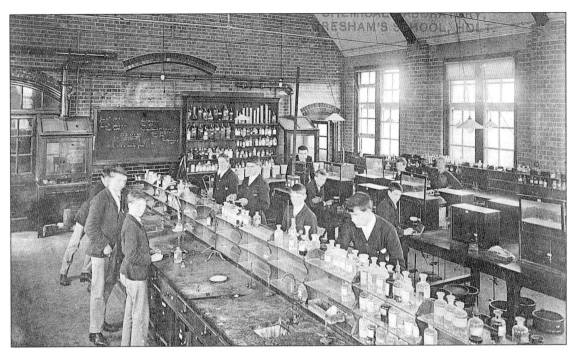

GRESHAM'S SCHOOL, HOLT, c. 1918

Gresham's School is one of Holt's most famous buildings. In this picture the pupils can be seen studying in the Chemical Laboratory. Sir John Gresham founded the school in 1555, being originally situated in the town centre. It later became a public boarding school and a new building was erected along the Cromer Road, opening in 1903. Amongst Greshams many distinguished boys were composer Benjamin Britten and poet W. H. Auden.

AYLSHAM POST OFFICE, c. 1914

The soldiers proudly posing for this picture are members of the South Wales Mounted Brigade of Despatch Riders. They were stationed at Aylsham during the First World War from 1914 to 1915. The post office was in this building from 1st January, 1893 until 1934. Once home to the International Stores, the premises are now occupied by Somerfields Food Stores.

RED LION STREET, AYLSHAM

BARNWELLS SERIES.

RED LION STREET, AYLSHAM, c. 1914

Looking down Red Lion Street during the First World War shows soldiers engaged in conversation and children posing for the camera. A variety of shops, advertising signs and the Cross Keys public house, which closed around 1920, can be seen on the right of the picture. Another public house was the Red Lion, which gave its name to Aylsham's main street and is probably one of the oldest inns in the town, dating back to 1700. Other inns in Red Lion Street were, the Bull 1839, which closed in 1906, the New Inn which was demolished in 1955, and The Star. A Working Men's Club and Institute in Red Lion Street is mentioned in a directory of 1879.

NORTH WALSHAM PARADE, c. 1908

Parading through the town centre with banner raised are the North Walsham branches of the Loyal Trafalgar Lodge of the Independent Order of Odd Fellows and the Manchester Unity Friendly Society. These movements were formed when the Combination Acts disallowed the forming of trade unions. The Friendly Societies provided help for members who had fallen upon hard times and suffered ill health. At one time there were approximately 500 people who were members in various town branches.

POLICE STATION, NORTH WALSHAM.

NORTH WALSHAM POLICE STATION, c. 1914

The Police Station at North Walsham is a red brick building built in 1903. It was also home to the Petty Sessional Court House and County Court. Prior to this, the police station was in Vicarage Street staffed by two constables and a Superintendent Lovick. The building to the left of the picture was later demolished and a new police station was erected on the site.

WITTON BRIDGE POST OFFICE, c. 1904

Witton Bridge is not far from where our journey began at Mundesley. The activity on the postcard indicates that at one time Witton Post Office was a very busy place. In 1890, Charles Cole was the postmaster, shopkeeper and pork butcher. George Sidney Savage was next to carry on the business from 1937. The last owner was a Mr. Beechcroft with the shop and post office being managed by Mr. Charles and Sally Owles and Mrs. London. The message on the reverse of this card reads: "Have sent you the post office but I am afraid it is no use to you for you cannot post your letters in it. Love Victoria". The business closed in June 1988 and is now a private dwelling.